THE
SAVAGE
COLONISER
BOOK

THE
SAVAGE
COLONISER
BOOK

Tusiata Avia

TE HERENGA WAKA
UNIVERSITY PRESS

Te Herenga Waka University Press
PO Box 600, Wellington
New Zealand
teherengawakapress.co.nz

A catalogue record is available at the National Library of New Zealand.

ISBN 9781776564095

Printed by Blue Star, Wellington, New Zealand

Acknowledgements
Some poems in this book first appeared in publications including
The Moth, *The Spinoff*, Phantom Billstickers, poetryshelf.co.nz
and *Ko Aotearoa Tātou / We Are New Zealand,* edited by Michelle Elvy,
Paula Morris and James Norcliffe (Otago University Press, 2020).
Apologies to the editors of any publications I may have missed.

For my tupu'aga: those who have gone before me
– foremost, my father, Namulau'ulu Mikaio Avia
(1929–2016) – and those who will come after.

<>

'Protest is telling the truth in public . . . We use
our bodies, our words, our art and our sounds both
to tell the truth about the pain we endure and to
demand the justice that we know is possible.'
—DeRay Mckesson, *On the Other Side of Freedom*

'Colonies are the outhouses of the European soul,
where a fellow can let his pants down and relax,
enjoy the smell of his own shit.'
—Thomas Pynchon, *Gravity's Rainbow*

E logo le tuli ona tātā.
The deaf hear when they are reminded.
—Samoan proverb

Contents

<>

<>

Savage   Coloniser Pantoum

This is a dumb game.
                    You can only lose.
You will die later in the night
you are a savage coloniser.

                    You can only lose.
This is a dumb game
you are a savage coloniser.
                    You are a dumb savage.

This is a dumb game.

                    You are a dumb waiter
                    you are a dumb savage
                    you have a shrunken head.

                    You are a dumb waiter.
You are a wooden servant.
                    You have a shrunken head.
This is a dumb down.

You are a wooden servant
you are a cut tree
this is a dumb down
this is a dumb game.

        You can only lose.

250th anniversary of James Cook's arrival in New Zealand

Hey James,
yeah, you
in the white wig
in that big *Endeavour*
sailing the blue, blue water
like a big arsehole
FUCK YOU, BITCH.

James,
I heard someone
shoved a knife
right up
into the gap between
your white ribs
at Kealakekua Bay.
I'm gonna go there
make a big Makahiki luau
cook a white pig
feed it to the dogs
and FUCK YOU UP, BITCH.

Hey James,
it's us.
These days
we're driving round
in SUVs
looking for ya
or white men like you
who might be thieves
or rapists
or kidnappers

or murderers
yeah, or any of your descendants
or any of your incarnations
cos, you know
ay, bitch?
We're gonna FUCK YOU UP.

Tonight, James,
it's me
Leilani, Danielle
and a car full of brown girls
we find you
on the corner
of the Justice Precinct.

You've got another woman
in a headlock
and I've got my father's
pig-hunting knife
in my fist
and we're coming to get you
sailing round
in your *Resolution*
your *Friendship*
your *Discovery*
and your fucking *Freelove*.

Watch your ribs, James
cos, I'm coming with
Kalaniōpuʻu
Kānekapōlei
Kanaʻina
Keaweʻōpala
Kūkaʻilimoku

who is a god
and Nua'a
who is king with a knife.

And then
James,
then
we're gonna
FUCK.
YOU.
UP.
FOR.
GOOD.
BITCH.

Listening to Tame

Tame says breathe.
It only took me eighteen years of my life
I'm used to this, the abuse
from you
the Pākehā

Sleep –
leave through the top of your soul
When they lock you up
let it go
the anger in your belly

We're all actors
It's a gun
It's a moment
It's a flag
I bought it from the $2 shop

It's not about how big my bum is
The system, it points its bum at you
every day
It's a moment
It's art

The *Urewera* is me
I am the *Urewera*
Papatūānuku is our mum
The wording
The wording
The wording
The wording

What does it mean?
My red? My blue?
The collaboration with the enemy?
Do you put it in the corner and have a mimi on it?

If you go round in Indonesia
you hear people say *taringa*.
It's whakapapa
We take care of the manuhiri
Somalians and people like yourself

(I used to say)
Wa wa wa wa wa
What the hell are you doing?
We all have a dream
Let's put it on the table
and have a cup of tea

I have 6000 mānuka
I've been down on my knees
planting these moko every day
Tch tch tch tch tch.

Jacinda Ardern goes to the Pacific Forum in Tuvalu and my family colonises her house

It's a nice new two-story house in South Auckland with a village in the backyard

I'm guessing that village doesn't actually belong to Jacinda and her family, but they have full use of it

We've been upstairs in Jacinda's house and we've made a bit of a mess really, it's all the kids

Who can stop them from dancing and dropping food on the floor which gets ground into the carpets?

I know Jacinda – who is the prime minister – we're all on first-name basis in this country, which is similar to Tuvalu where their prime minister is sitting on the roof of his house

I know Jacinda is weary, it's hot over there in Tuvalu and tiring because the sea is taking over, so, now the only place to play cricket is the airport runway

And the school kids have to sit cross-legged in their classrooms up to their waists in seawater, but they still wear their uniforms proudly with that lovely shiny black hair that Island kids have

It's a crisis all right, but it's also tiring and Jacinda goes back to her house which she paid for out of her prime minister money

We all know that her partner does a lot of the child-care, but you can't tell me that it's not tiring to be a prime minister of a whole country and have a baby as well

It must be nearly as tiring as being a Tuvaluan prime minister sitting on his own roof to stop from drowning

I feel sorry for Jacinda because I'm a solo mother and know how tiring working and looking after a baby can be

I want to advise her to get a nanny, I know I'd get a nanny so I could get some sleep, if I had as much money as a prime minister

I'm not sure how angry she is about my family having colonised her house, but she does look stressed and not like she does on TV

She's trying to think of something to say over the sound of my family – who are talking to each other across the wide spaces, because it's a really big house that she's got here – when she says to me:

Yes, there's something about the Polynesian accent that makes the things you're saying sound really threatening

While I'm trying to come up with the next thing to say, I hear the voices of a whole lot of cuzzies I haven't seen for ages. They're walking around and sitting down and taking over the village. Ihumātao village. Right here in her backyard.

Burnt Australia fair

You said we weren't here.
Cockatoos can only stay in the sky for so long

till they swoop down to terra nullius like burning fighter
planes. Dragons fly round their own circular songlines –

it's a warning.
Sing the words: _____

Yeah, you know the words, do ya?
The words are gone now, mate

our tongues were burnt to ashes long before.
White fella houses go up in smoke.

They start living in caravans
like they're the dispossessed.

Sing the words: _____
take these bad dreams away

hook them to the sharp beaks of burnt cockatoo
and fly them away from here.

Cook, you bastard
we've been hungry and angry and murdered for a long time.

The Pacific solution

Put all the refugees on Manus
They will sew their mouths up red
Kill themselves on concrete floors
There in Pasifika mecca.

They will sew their mouths up red
Put all the refugees on Nauru
There in Pasifika mecca
Every island Jerusalem.

Put all the refugees on Nauru
Slash their throats and watch the sun
Every island Jerusalema
Close their eyes in the island sun.

Slash their throats and watch the sun
Watch their children die beside them
Close their eyes in the island sun.
Fair Australia will guard them closely and

Put all the refugees on Manus.

Fucking St Barbara (i)

What happens when you fall for an Australian goldmine?
I'm not speaking in metaphors here, I mean:
the mechanics, the walls, the maintenance
the stock exchange for the March 31 quarter
the whole St Barbara Company Ltd who own
the island economy on Simberi
the 1100 indigenous people
the Cape Coloureds brought over from South Africa
who look like The Rock but with 2 grams of gold per tonne of earth.

Corporate responsibilities stop in the hole
between my legs. You've got to dig a big hole
to get to the ore body
you might even have to remove a mountain
and then dig another big hole in the ground
the size of twenty-one football fields
to get to this ore body's ass.

How long can I keep his hands off?
How long?
Where can I hide?
Inside the water?
Even the sea is full of rapists.

He prowls a mile under the surface of my skin
He has large grinding wheels in his cock
it rips me up like I'm concrete, like I'm the sea floor.

He wins the St Barbara 2020 Digger of the Year award
for his performance: 93,000 Ounces of Gold out of Simberi.
He kisses me before his walk to the podium
as they play 'You Ain't Seen Nothing Yet'.

Fucking St Barbara (ii)

In the centre of Simberi Island the trees have created a woman
the goddess comes out of the ground there

St Barbara says the local culture is wicked like that
the local people leave gorgor leaves to warn her off

they leave them hanging over the yellow bars around the pit
leave them outside the solid silver doors

this is where St Barbara and her children
will be cut up into pieces and thrown across the floor.

Poly kidz r coming

Boom Shakalaka Shirley Boys are dressed in pink
sharp teeth round their necks

> *Shirley-is-a-girl's-name!*
> *Where's your boyfriend?*

Their taupou is a boy with muscles
chanting:

> *Shirley Boys is coming!*
> *Where's your boyfriend?*

<>

Marlborough Boys are flying Tongans
bicking all da crapes
Marlborough Girls are britty kirls
bicking all da crapes
All da islands to da vineyards
bicking all da crapes
Tonga, Sāmoa, Tokelau
bicking all da crapes
Tuvalu, Niue, PNG
bicking all da crapes

<>

Suga, you wanna fofō? You gonna lie on my table an write da
boem? Apout me? I gotta send money to my fricken family in
Sāmoa. Don worry, no Corona here, I put da cover for your
mouf.

21

See dat taupou? She frow da gaifi up da air and no one catch!
Da boy behind her not even look, just too busy look around all
da kirls. Might be cut da head off. He's from my family. What
a stupid!

<>

The Tongan boys salute and march and cut us with their spears
Tongan mama gets up on stage
red feathers behind her ear
Marlborough vintage on her feet
Mama takes the spear

Cheehoooooooooo!

We scream

Cheehoooooooooo!

They will rule us like an army

Watch out Marlborough, Tongan Boys are coming
Where's your girlfriend?

<>

Christchurch Samoan girls go

tik tok
tik tok

Throw themselves down on the floor

tik tok
tik tok

The spirits of aiuli enter

tik tok
tik tok

We scream and laugh
and eat chop suey

Cheeehooooo!

<>

Bro says, Don't kiss and hug, pretend like you're The Rock, just raise your eyebrow. Remember Corona and measles and the 1918 influenza.

The Villa Girls dance 1918 and die like flies on stage.

I wanna be head girl next year, Mum
                     all eyes on me
                            I wanna be the taupou, Mum
Dancing in the middle
                  Centre. Of. Attention.

<>

We're looking at the white people when they walk past us and it's just different today, ay? We're in the red zone, but it's like the Brown Zone in Christchurch today, ay?

                Yeah, uce, we *are* the Brown Zone.

<>

Cheehoooooo!

Poly kidz are coming
Where's your vineyard?
Poly kidz are coming
Where's your white zone?

Martin Luther King Day

Alien no. 2017999
vomits through the tracheostomy hole in his neck
down his front to his manacled feet
down to the lilies of the field.
These, too, belong to us.

Dear Martin,
A wind is rising.
While you were, of course
speaking your own way,
I will repeat this:
uplift, defend the struggle
for voting rights.
No to segregation.
I shall have more to say
when I see you.
As soon as I feel you
have received this letter
I will call you.

Gifted and black
open your heart
souls intact.
Young, gifted and black.

Those of us who are gathered here today
honour a man who was shot and killed.

The tenets America was founded on:
gun rights
I Am OK Day
police in riot gear
plantocracy paved the way.

Swing the Richmond, Virginia dance.
Democrats dance
like conservatives.
The red dance
the blue dance.

Wall Street goes to both parties and dances.
Left party?
There is no left party
(all the true believers leave).
Mr Duopoly –
we don't know what he stands for.
Clouds in the room
fill the dance floor.

Soldiers hide in the clouds.
The boy who never asked for this
holds on for the earthquakes
in Puerto Rico.
Hurricane Maria
dancing dancing
here comes destruction
dancing dancing.

No one's gonna come for us
get your backpack on.
When the power goes out what happens
to Gramma's dialysis machine?
Destruction party
colony party
referendum party
but no one is listening.
Mass party
incarceration party.

Slaveocracy wins the day.
You can't charity us away.
No one ever makes a billion $
they take a billion $.
It's all gonna get cut and clipped.
Biting edges make the helipad.
Helipad party
oil party
widget party.

Gifted and black
open your heart
souls intact.
Young, gifted and black.

Alexandria Ocasio-Cortez:
When I first walked into the party
I saw my name-plaque on the door
I thought, I'm not supposed to be here.
Marshawn Lynch:
When I got my first pair of Jordans
I thought, I'm not meant to be here
I'll pay for this later.

I'm in the bathroom and
my hair is falling out.
(Lupus is an autoimmune disease
caused by stress).
All we have is each other.

Don't get complacent –
I want some seconds
and some thirds and fourths.
Out of the muddy waters

I need shelter.

Who's fighting, who's dying
and who's dying for the cause?
Millions of dollars spent every day
to hold the troops
in South Vietnam
and our country
cannot protect the rights
of Negroes in Selma.

Those of us who are gathered here today
honour a man who was shot and killed.

The whole Jericho road must be transformed.
Approach death with wisdom, justice and bruised hands.

Gifted and black
open your heart
souls intact.
Young, gifted and black.

Go into a hostile world.
Every low place shall be made high.
The moving finger writes
and having written, moves on.
Justice will roll down the waters
and righteousness
like the mighty stream.

Barbara Jordan:
You want more than a recital of problems.
(This small black woman filled the cathedral of America.)
As I would not be a slave, so I would not be a master.

The principal party
the president party.
We will not wait for the president.
I say, we will not wait for the president!
We will pursue our own scorched earth policy
burn Jim Crow to the ground.

Those of us who are gathered here today
honour a man who was shot and killed.

I've been gone for a little while
at least my body's been gone.
But I'm back now.
And we got another hill to climb.

BLM

I'm looking straight into the camera
My ancestors standing behind me
I'm holding my hands in my pockets
I'm holding my knee on his neck

My ancestors standing behind me
White knights in a long line behind me
I'm holding my knee on his neck
This is the way that we do it

White knights in a long line behind me
Shout, *Look into the camera with pride*
This is the way that we do it
This is your God-given right

Look into the camera with pride
Kneel like a prayer full of lynching
This is my God-given right
Crushing the head of the black man.

Kneel like a prayer full of lynching
Behold the power of God
Crushing the head of the black man
This is my God-given white.

Behold the power of God
Holding my hands in my pockets
Ancestors kneeling to join me
We're looking straight into the camera.

Massacre

Thursday 14 March

When I arrive in Auckland and Hine learns
that I have moved back to Christchurch
she asks me if I know it is a bad place
it is built on a swamp
many bad things have been done to Māori there.

Yes, I tell her and remember standing, six years old
in the hallway, the swamp spirits rising up through the floor.
Walking to school through them
sitting beside them on the bus.

Friday 15 March

The white spirits rise up from the swamp
and many bad things happen
the white spirits rise up from the swamp and kill
those who kneel and pray
and stand
and walk and run
and punch the windows out with their bare hands
and drag themselves through the glass
and stumble and fall
and find the body of a boy
and close his eyes
and take his cellphone from his hand
and tell his mother screaming through it
that her son is dead
and then they stand again
and run and run and run and run.

We, white men who have carved ourselves into statues
and guard the four avenues, rise
we, Queen Victoria – made of stone – who stares into the air
past every kind of massacre, rise
we, far right, we rise
we, skinheads, we rise
we, the white supreme, we rise

we are white ghosts and we rise up out of the swamp.
You cry and shake as if the earthquake is coming
but we are not here for you.

We are here for the three-year-old Muslim boy
for the 71-year-old Muslim man
for the 45-year-old Muslim man
and his 16-year-old son
for the 44-year-old Muslim woman
the 65-year-old grandmother
the 14-year-old Muslim boy
the 25-year-old Muslim woman.
We are here for 101 Muslims
we are not here for you.

You can lock down your schools and your buildings
and your pain can come and go
but we don't care, we have not come here for you.

We will not chase you through Hagley Park
we are here on holy day Friday for Al Noor Mosque.
We will not chase you through Eastgate Mall
we are here on holy day Friday for Linwood Masjid.

We are only killing the people you have been calling the terrorists
and today, we look like *Fortnight*.

Sunday 17 March

I watch Jacinda at Al Noor after many bad things happen
she is in a black and gold hijab
she says many things but – she has her hand over her heart
she keeps it there.

The spirits have sunk back out of sight
you are watching that 'individual' from Australia
you are saying to me: He isn't us.

But I grew up with him
he was Eddie the skinhead in my science class
everybody knew him
he had a Māori girlfriend for a while
and wore a Nazi trench coat which you told me was cool.

Remember, you grew up with him
he was Danny, not in your class
because he was younger than you
but you watched him walk through the playground
with his bootboy boots and his swastikas.

It was Christchurch – and all the other places –
back when you were young
and it was cool and it was the fashion
it was the fashion and you and I were into it.

Friday 22 March

In Auckland I sit at the vigil
the women of Ngāti Whātua call to the sacred land
across Tāmaki Makaurau

33

the women call to the martyrs, to the broken-hearted
the women do the grieving for us
the women remind us of Parihaka and Ruatoki
the murdered and their murderers.

The women say
that they have been fighting since Captain Cook landed
and after they grieve, they will fight.

A white man who could be scary in another place
hands me a sign and I take it.
It says 'NZ was founded on White Supremacist Violence'.
He looks into my eyes, I nod and hoist it to my shoulder.

I watch a white woman weep and tell me it is hard to be white
I read a poet say he feels the shame
of talking about how he feels.

A white poet can only talk about how he feels
I can only talk about how I feel
I can only weep like the white woman
and write you this poem that will not end

Man in the wheelchair

When I arrived at the airport in 1988
I waited only 40 minutes for a stranger
from Western Sāmoa
he took me to a priest's house
who took me to a Sikh's house.

Can I sleep in your bed?
Can I come to your church?
Can I pray in your office?

When I was young, I listen to a story from my teacher.
By the time I open my eyes . . .

<>

full metal-jacketed bullets travelling through the bodies
semi-jacketed bullets 'lead snowstorming' through the bodies
semi-jacketed bullets releasing numerous small lead fragments
through the bodies
careening bullets entering through the skulls and travelling
through the heads
tangential bullets obliquely striking the bodies
penetrating projectiles bouncing off the inner tables of the skulls
ricocheting bullet fragments spreading along the bullet course
inside the bodies
penetrating bullets entering the bodies with no exit wounds
in the bodies
perforating bullets entering with tract and exiting
through the bodies.

<>

You cannot bribe the angels
even they cannot kill the racism.

I have the feeling of suicidal.
So, I go behind the hospital unit in the bush
and I scream and cry.

Do not kill yourself.
Who gave you permission?
Stand up even against yourself
by the weight of an atom.
Do not cut down the fruit-bearing bush.

I don't want to be like a volcano.
That is why I have chosen
love, peace, forgiveness.
Oh God, open the door for all New Zealand.

White power

i
I board a white plane / seat 2A / Sorry miss / you need to go
down to the back / into the white power row /

ii
My neighbour punches me in the face / and then / again / and
then he wrecks me / as the others watch / and I disappear /

ii [Replay]
She boards the plane / seat 2A / The pilot himself comes out
and says: This seat is reserved for the rich white man / who
is not travelling today / but just in case he does / and out of
respect for him / you need to go down to the back /

They are half out of their seats / her killer and his colleagues
/ they have some interesting tattoos / and even though they
will kill her soon / she notices how / they don't look how she
expects / they look like an indie-folk band / Her neighbour
kills her /

iii
My killer and I continue to another place / this is not Heaven
/ it's just the inside of a house / The longer we are here / the
darker he becomes / I take his face in my hands and say: The
more you kill me, the more you kill yourself /

iv
He is Ethiopian now / Are you Ethiopian? I say / He nods /
I take his face in my hands again and say: You are back home
where you began / priests are carrying copies of the ark to
Lalibela / there are many copies of the Covenant / you are
carrying a velvet umbrella / to protect them from the sun /

Many people are dancing / God is here / your face is shining / you are singing and / Amharic is coming out of your mouth.

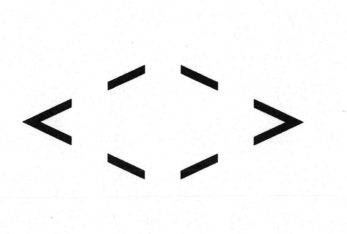

We talk about sex poems

You tell me about a pair of women's underwear
fluttering from a military installation,
the lacy knickers waving a surrender or a covert revolution maybe.
It's hard to write well about sex. And heartache.

I need someone a little bit broken to hold me tonight
while the party rages opposite, while Dominic strips down
to his underwear and shows everyone his tattoos:
Pain equals progress. The way his bones are breaking down too.

I ask what you want – it's been a long time
and I don't know the terrain of your body.
You don't ask for anything
but say things the grown children of explorers might.

Now, I want to stop, switch on all the lights
deprive my own nerve endings
so my eyes can lick you like a sweet-toothed cartographer
then store you away carefully, carefully in special paper.

There are many hollows in the body where water could be held
the clavicles, the indentations in the belly,
the spaces between the ribs –
long cool glass of water is a dumb thing to say so I keep it quiet –
the reverberations in a cave.

When there is more space – a room's length now –
I open my eyes wide.
Your legs are too long for metaphors
your ass some inconceivably high and unnamed planet.
There are bullet-holes too, from Trinidad and Tobago maybe,
the US, Blackwater maybe.

I need someone a little bit broken
so, put your fingers high up inside me
and rock me like you would a cradle.
I drown out the sounds of the party and the poetry
and the crows outside these hotel windows.

I don't know where these things flew from or what sadness
they brought with them, but I saw an ibis
bobbing through the mall outside the always-empty Nepali
restaurant that sells twenty-one types of parmigiana.
It will be OK, there is enough of the sacred here.

There are moments in the dark under your weight
when I know my hip-bones are much closer to the surface
than the last time I lay like this with a man.
In the morning I hold you for the last time.
It has taken nine years from first kiss to this.

Let me hold you, lover, because in nine years I'll be sixty
and you will be nearly three score and ten
and the hollowing out that has begun on both our beauties
will have taken us into a new kind of broken.

I have seen statues like you: Ramses and other rulers
and I have entered buildings and heard people gasp
and leap to their feet as if they should.
And I've swept out again in my Rasta queen dress with the train.

I have spent a good deal of my sex life
soothing my manifold partners
but for you, this soothing soothes me too
soothes my hollowing, the way my flesh has fallen from me
the way it reminds me of my father's
the way his bones rose like nature's excavation of fossils

once all the flesh has gone and all the earth
that covered the bones has gone too.

It is at the door, after we have said goodbye,
after I have closed the door
and you have walked away down the hall like Ramses
that my broken breaks open.
Great fissures run through me
into the floor, down past the lift shaft
and through the underworld into Fortitude Valley.

I am in hospital after another seizure

I wake up to my life continuing
and to neurosurgeons and their students, talking about it.
Teddy Woo turns away from me and says to the nurse
'She is riddled with them'
and then uses words:

acoustic neuroma
astrocytoma
glioblastoma
craniopharyngioma
brainstem glioma
ependymoma
medulloblastoma
oligodendroglioma.

It is frightening but it is something
and something is something more than
the shrugging of Teddy Woo's shoulders
I chase him around the bed and beg him for more info
Teddy Woo, I say to him, Teddy Woo.

Acanthogonatus
acanthoscurria
avicularia
brachypelma
chaetopelma
ceratogyrus
grammostola
hysterocrates.

These are all names for spiders.
There is one on the ceiling.

The round swollen belly of a spider
could be the back of the head of a neurosurgeon.
My children are terrified of him.
When he climbs down off the ceiling I say
'Look, kids, it's just a neurosurgeon.'

Two hundred neurosurgeons are gathering
for congress in my city.
One of them became a neurosurgeon
to rid herself of her fear of spiders.
There are neurologists that can spend
up to nineteen days underwater
they are all around the seashore during your sunset walks
you just haven't noticed them.

Ma‘i maliu (i)

I lie on the floor in corpse pose. I have been dead for three weeks now. Audrey and Ben enter their house to find me on their floor.

I measure myself against 23-kilometre races that I'm not running. Up Mt Vaea with a TV crew at my back – all the amazing stories I'm not talking about, the selfies I'm not jostling to be in, set against a Samoan sunset. See look, I'm not there. See look, I'm not telling the stories, I'm not winning this or writing that. I don't even know if I'm writing this poem. Maybe I'll write this poem and then I'll forget.

I lie on the floor in corpse pose. I find myself on a hotel bathroom floor just before the book awards. I ring my cousin in Christchurch to ask where I am. I ring Catherine to come and get me. I ring Selina to stand behind me on the stage just in case. The next morning they find me dead in the breakfast bar. Catherine's face looms over me as the ambulance arrives. I get all death-bed on her and tell her I love her. I touch her cheek and afterwards don't know why. I guess that's what you do when you are dying.

Perhaps I'm getting deader all the time or perhaps I want to use this poem to explain to you why I'm not writing. Why I shuffle through the day from death pose to death pose. The bits in between are not marathons, they're not novels or poems, they're not even driving a car. Dead people aren't allowed to drive cars.

<>

I wake up with dead people pulling me down the hall. I fight my girl into her clothes, cut toast, forget I'm in the kitchen. Brush my girl's hair. She gets angry because I'm not specific, I say 'thingy' all the time.

The doctor told me the pills would ruin my word recall – and he wanted to double the dose. *You can't do that*, I said, *I'm writing a* book. *OK, then, I'll triple them*, he said.

I show the pills to my daughter and explain why I say 'thingy' all the time. *But I can't see it happening, Mummy*, she says. I nag her to get her thingys on and then she's gone. I sit on the couch. Forget my father is dead. Then remember. Then I cry.

This is called *jamais vu*. It's not dying – it's the opposite of *déjà vu*. *Déjà vu* feels like having memories before you have them. *Jamais vu* feels like forgetting your father is dead and then remembering and then crying.

Ma'i maliu (ii)

It starts with losing my footing – the way a person does in an earthquake, when the floor becomes the sea. I fall and slide headlong into the corner, where the linen cupboard meets the bathroom. I am face up, pulled along by the torpedo of my head.

A pile of coat hangers pierce the top of my head, my forehead and the top of my face and narrowly miss my eyes. Perhaps they stake out an area of my brain, the punctures like stitching, like a diagram in a 1950s neurology text.

My handsome untouchable father walks up the hallway. He beams above me and I beg him, I cry and cry for fifty years. But he is thirty, and he looks somewhere above me, smiling and talking to someone else.

I've had a seizure, Dad. I choke this out, but I am speaking into space. When I am on my feet I turn back to the corner and there is my blood halo on the wall.

If I look at myself in the bathroom mirror I am there. There are my wounds, not gory, just there. And there is my face, paler than I've seen it, thinner, so I don't look as much like me as I should.

My mother has been watching quietly but is gone. I try to track her, making my way past the old chicken farm that used to be behind the house, then the big tree, the rope swing hanging from it.

She is sitting there. I see her in three-quarter profile. She is crying. My mother's tears come only three times a lifetime and they are silent and strike me hard in the chest. I step back into the shadow but I am forty or fifty years old so I step forward again.

I don't look or speak but I sit down beside her. I hook my arm through hers and press my knee against her knee. I exist and I can help.

Every seizure a dating opportunity

I have a seizure in my sleep and wake
in a pool of urine. It smells as if I've swum
through a tunnel in the Red Sea reef
and come up into your bedroom
with my tongue bitten because you're such a rough lover.

At the Pacific Arts Conference in Hawai'i
I finger you under a table
in the middle of an argument with the head honcho.
She holds up her middle finger as a fuck-you
and runs her pointer back and forth over her chubby thumb.

I ignore the fact that you are still leaking
really slowly, but leaking and ignoring it.
Apart from that you are really good-looking and sexy as.

After you've finger-fucked me
two fingers, then three or four
all arguments over
I give you the keys to my room.

During the plenary I imagine myself ringing you
with a desperate kind of feeling
and you telling me you probably won't be back.
I close my eyes and whisper my spell:
Every seizure a dating opportunity.

Environmental sex

There is a man in my bed, which is as extraordinary as me
leaping into the air in the shape of Grace Jones
in *Island Life* and staying there, suspended.

I can do it
I can do yoga
I have seen Circe de Soleil.

He is so surprised in my hole
he is so surprised in there
something really ordinary can be made into something else –

warty labiatus into blobfish
mudpuppy into milksnake
spotless axolotl into hellbender.

No, you cannot eat the deep waters off New Zealand.
You cannot eat this currently endangered species.

Digital sex

Here is one thing I've learned: if the French are after you,
fall in alongside the Russians when they come.
Remember there are still Ethiopian police
wearing the old Soviet greatcoats in the heat of a district
you have never heard of, they are still
keeping the peace dressed like that.
March home with them, don't be fussy
even about living in an ice-cave if that's where they live.
Even if your shoes are soaked through, take them off –
you'll be surprised how ice heats up when full of bodies.
You think you can demand your way out? You think
you've earned it? You think they're not your captors too?
In the end a soldier in a greatcoat is just a boy in wool.
Any army splits off into factions,
no boy band can stay together,
gymnasts don't last but they can still do forward rolls
when they're old. Everyone is going to want what they want
from you, even if it contravenes your rights.
Get used to the way things are in ice-caves.
Run next door if you can, yes, you can make it,
run somewhere further down the road.
Ha! Looks like an ice cave in there too, doesn't it?
Maybe just go with it. Don't be surprised when you wake up
masturbating under an empty pile of greatcoats.
Discover a gymnast's fingers are finer and more dextrous
than anything you could imagine, like fucking
in the warm waters of the Blue Nile,
which runs straight into Sudan.
Life's just not as straightforward as it seemed
at the beginning of this poem
and there are a lot of weird people
I would have digital sex with if given a chance.

Jason

Jason says mmmm like in those uncomfortable online dating
chats with no punctuation
Jason is a plasterer and likes dogs and good English pubs.
Jason's neck is as thick as one of those scary dogs
who savage babies' faces off
and chase you screaming up the roads of Peckham.

You can follow Jason on Google Maps –
he's made it into the photograph at the front of your
Nigerian ex-boyfriend's house.
Jason's in a hoody with his face blurred out
and telltale white dust on his hands
you can zoom up close and spot it.

Jason, go to the High Street
and buy deep-fried black bananas
and eat them with five-meat stew.
Now Go Back to the House, you shout at Google Maps
so I can see the open door on Furley Street and my ex
looking twenty years older.
So much like my father now (it was bound to happen).
This is what I've been waiting for, Jason
all my life, all my life.

Let's watch him through the window, Jason,
creep in and wait with the furniture
(it's cold in there, his father in Nigeria wants to save money).
See the walls, they are still green
they could be velvet or a forest if you hold your eyes like 1999.

The furniture is curved like a cervix
and there on the floor is a Poise

my ex is incontinent now, but we should always protect him.
Jason, you dumb-dumb, just move it
into the corner with your foot.

When I think about this my eyes tear up
till Jason taps me on my virtual shoulder.
I've missed the wedding guests file in.
And my ex's new wife in her dress.

The Peckham light is bouncing off the estate opposite
no one is throwing you out, Jason.
No one is noticing me either.

Tyrone

At eight years old
his shiny, floppy hair
his holey jersey and little boy shorts
this is before he's hurt anyone.
He wanders into the pub, pushes his hair out of his eyes
and looks up at us.
There is a woman on the dance floor dancing dirty
he will grow up fast and everyone will be ruined.

Tyrone's wife screams back
Fuck ya muthafucka!
He holds her down, hand on her throat
he pulls back his fist
punches so exactly
she feels the wind in her hair
before he opens up the floor.

We rest on the bar, we finger our keys, we bargain for a while.
The moon is out, it's gonna be a hell of a night.

<>

Tyrone's car tyres are not only flat but slashed open. They're
not tyres. They're symbols of his heart. Everything inside him
is hanging out. The hard stuff has spilt the soft stuff and there
is no patching up.

Tyrone guesses it's best to stay here with the young and
unpatched, the soon-to-be proper criminals, the Mongols
flying in from Australia. The Mongols have already burnt
down the barbers beside Pak'nSave, the one across the road
from the church that has the sign saying

Do you want Jesus inside you? That's the same church that the man who hid those dead bodies under his floorboards went to. His house got burnt down too, but long before the Mongols got here.

Yeah, he's violent

But you knew he was. And he won't let you take your meds – we all know you're addicted. But, you don't buy them on the street or anything. I'll smuggle you two pills, you know he'll count them.

Cuz, we have a head-start on him, leave everything behind. Come on, let's go!

Gotta say, this place is flash though. I'm surprised Aunty's house turned out so good. I'm surprised she even let us stay here. It's better than the old one, but she's still a fucken bitch. They've even got a pool.

Yep, yep, I will stop fucking around.

Fucken hell, cuz, did you see that?

No, not your stink boyfriend. One of his āiga jumped out of the bush. I was just having a quick goodbye dip. Didn't you see the way he went under with my high heel stuck in the side of his neck?

Quickest way out of here is taxi. Of course my loser ex is the driver. Got to be another way out of here.

Nope, I've never seen a Swiss chick in this village.

I don't know what she looks like. Just, her hair is white like a flag. Not a surrender flag, one of those lifeguard ones.

The bus she's driving is ancient, straight out of Basra.

What's the name of my village? Whatever Guantanamo is in Samoan.

Go, go, Swiss chick!

Jesus, not down the ravine, this chick is crazy! Just hold on, cuz, or you'll pitch out those blown-out windows.

Look, Uncle's on the other side, outside the church. You know he's waiting for us, ay?

Talofa Uncle, ua lelei mea uma. Yep, everything is good.

Cuz! Can't you see, that's the brother of that guy I drowned? Watching me from behind the church?

And the full moon is out. It'd be a lovely night if this shit wasn't happening.

Jealousy (i)

I'm jealous of _____, whenever I hear his amazing work full of images that blow everyone's mind / I paste a smile on my face in case someone is watching me (I'm convinced someone is always watching me) / and even though it comes close to blowing my mind too / I can't let it / I know it's brilliant / but I can't feel it or laugh like everyone else here / who is open and generous / not full of jealousy like I am.

I've met _____ just a couple of times / he didn't smile at me or even speak / he limply shook my hand so I could hardly feel it, like: You're so not a good poet / you're old/ and I am so fire right now.

I'm jealous of _____ , so when my eleven-year-old turns to me during _____'s reading and says: What even was that? / and: You should've won that prize / I hold her to me with a fierce gratitude and pride and guilt.

Jealousy (ii)

I listen to Eckhart Tolle every day / sometimes he's talking to Oprah to really break it down to me like I'm Christian middle America / when I'm listening I feel like a better person / like I'm above jealousy / like there is enough poetry applause for everyone / but sitting in _____'s audience it all comes sliding up and / I realise what a frightened person I am / how un-awakened I truly am.

Will I have to come back here in the next life and marry _____who will be famous again? / Will I have to listen to _____till all my jealousy leaves me? / With Eckhart and Oprah I'm sure I'm spiritually evolved enough not to have to come back to this veil of jealous-tears / I'll get to ascend to a higher tier of the wedding cake that is the afterlife/ maybe I'll get to enter through the welcome-good-and faithful entrance / where I'll get to lie around on celestial deck chairs and drink celestial cocktails served by celestial waiters / with those souls who are having to work out their jealousy and nastiness in comfort.

Maybe I'll become a Michael Landon spirit guide and come back to Earth to look after a lesser soul / I'll have to look after a soul, maybe like_____. Until I realise _____ is actually my spirit guide and I bear more resemblance to Laura Ingalls when she drowned her pet dog / The real Michael Landon guide will look on with detachment and spiritual evolution / because he has won many prizes for being a natural and super-talented angel.

FafSwag Spell (i)

TEINE SĀ:
I am the body>>>

WOMEN:
There is a space inside
our bodies the exact shape and size.
When we see you we say, *Look there I am*>>>

You dance
the taualuga topless like
the taualuga should be danced.
You are shining with luminous oil. We aiuli you.
We paper your precolonial body with NZ legal tender>>>

TEINE SĀ:
Tend to my precolonial
body, my body, my body, my body
tend to my body, tend to my body, tender
me, tender me, tender me, tender me, tender me
body me, body me, body me, body me, body me, body>>>

This is the spell:
Look for the space in my
body. It is lit by the maʻi aitu. Fire-
flies from Pulotu. Watch me slap myself
against the holy flesh. Watch me swallow the floor.
My white eyeballs. Once you see me, you cannot unsee>>>

WOMEN:
Tell me who you hate.
We hate them too. Look through
the layers of our limbs. These are your
thighslayers – fast-twitch muscle and fat meant
for crossing the cold salt sea, under the constellations,

executing the splits.
Don't exist us without you.
We hate everyone who hates you.
We are possessed by a ma'i aitu. We are possessed
by a ma'i maliu. We can fall. We can die any time>>>

FafSwag Spell (ii)

Akashi hands me the mic, this impossible bronze body –
rumour has it she trains in stilettos. Later in the night on the
rooftop I will tell her I met Grace Jones in New York City,
because she is a dead ringer and I will ask her if the physical
balance of training in heels helps with emotional balance. She
is twenty-two.

I take the mic – its phallic ceremony. Tamatoa is splayed at my
feet. FafSwag. I lead them in from the back. The bronze body
squats behind me. We stand in my shoes, the spell comes out
of my mouth.

Tamatoa dances out of the kava roots that grow out of the
ends of his hands. His beard is glittering black with shoe
polish. Aitu rise from the underworld, dance under the skin
of his arms – muscled with incubi, the unborn.

Akashi turns the crowd into her howl: *This is not a one-
way thing, motherfuckers! When a Bitch gives, you give back!*
FafSwag vogue us: runway, duckwalk, hands, pop-dip-and-
spin, tornado. They death-drop us and bring us back again.

And while we are snapping our finger bones, the aitu who lie
under this gallery are finally freed to push. Past the stacked
bodies of all the old white guys and their easels and their oils
extruded from the ground. *Come through!* we shriek. *Come
through!*

These trans-aitu have come a long way to penetrate these dead
men. All their graves are liquifacted now. Mafui'e, Samoan
god of earthquakes, pulls out his milky eyes and slides up
through Akashi the bronze, up through Falencie the fleshsex,

63

up through Tamatoa the rippling, up through Mistress Moe.

Mistress hunches like a Spanish Catholic, dipping and flicking, cleansing the whiteness away.

Akashi swoons in a net and a thong and I steady myself, the small of my back against the balcony rail.

And then, in frozen silence, I tip backwards. I execute the perfect death-drop. I watch myself fall slowly, slowly, seven storeys to the ground.

FafSwag Spell (iii)

for Falencie

You are the plane tilting and I feel the lift of the ground leaving.
It happens in the manava and it happens between the legs.

You are the two black wings stretched wide
with the body in between.

I am the incorporeal water suspended in the air.
I am the wishing.

Here comes my voice: what is the name in Samoan for the bird
with the outstretched wings?

If my father was alive I would ask him,
but like with everything now, I go inside.

<>

La Chana dances flamenco through the passages of her own
body, not the veins or capillaries but the spirit-corridors.
She dances with her eyes closed, sitting down
because she is old now, her eyes closed and her head to one side,
listening, fingers snapping.
She sits and she talks about the dance, the entrance,
the choosing without choosing. Then she goes inside and I weep
You are the ghost of the best flamenco dancer in Spain.

<>

This is an act of worship.
Falencie is worship
La Chana is worship
Possession is worship
Ma'i maliu is worship
Teine Sā is worship
Fatigue is worship
Flamenco shoes is worship
Hip is worship
Knees is worship
The torn meniscus is worship
Dead father is worship
All this inside, is inside my body and is worship.

<>

Wheel your wings like the bird I don't know the name of
hold the chaos of all your own pain.

See me falling down La Chana's stairs
my own meniscus underfoot.

See me falling, see them throwing me.
Teine Sā doesn't come empty, she comes full of Her

and she comes full of you and La Chana
and the nursing homes or hospital beds or tombs
we will end the dance in.

Blacking out the Vā (i)

In this legend the twins don't forget the words and women keep the peʻa.

O le malaga of the two who swam / fafine not tāne / the women not the men / vaʻaia, the clam!

Swim
$\qquad$ dive
$\qquad\qquad$ for the storehouse>>>

This time we remember the words / we sing the women not the men / we tatau fafine / we tattoo the women / not the men / pity the men / talofa e / alas the men / auē! / spearheads / vaʻa / faʻamuliʻaliao / centipedes / combs / wild bananas.

Flying
$\qquad$ fox
$\qquad\qquad$ fly.
Peʻa   for   the   women   not the men>>>

VĀ
is not empty.
Space
enters the space
enters the meaning
changes the creature.
Mana
VĀ
manava
mānava
breathe
VĀ
sā
sacred
ocean
Vasa
VĀnimonimo
everything appears
and disappears:
Āiga
Atua
The cosmos
Betweenness
Balance
Aptness
Rest
<<<
The   beautiful   order   was   never   erased.

Blacking out the Vā (iii)

One dark night
Samoan nakedness
arse and genitals
naked savages
ambushed the ashamed Victorians
conjured up
Samoan soga'imiti-women, tattooed in Aotearoa.
We called
let's go fight
let's go war
against the apt
the right
the proper
the fitting.
We will bite u
wring the juice
from your eggs.
We are upside-down atua
flying through the darkness
wings
       spread
           on our
               tatau.
                   See
                       the darkness
                             call to us,
                                 >>>
the   women.   Fa'alele   lau   pe'a.   Let   your   flying   fox   fly!

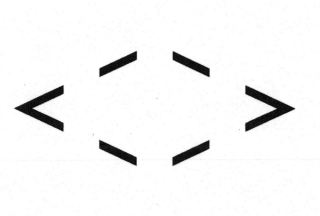

Covid in the time of Primeminiscinda

I'm not listening to Jacinda
I'm going to my friend's party and all the herbalists are there
listing all the things:
Thieves Oil, whiteywood, kānuka, honeysuckle, pōhutukawa,
horopito, elderberry syrup.
It's really easy, they say, all you have to do is go for many
miles into the wilds, recognise the right things, pick them,
dry them in a confusing and special way, boil them, decant
them, strain them into pure glass bottles and seal them.
You'll be lucky to find them for sale anymore.
This freaks me out so I go home.

Level 1

I'm listening to Jacinda
I'm telling myself that I'm staying the hell away from herbalists
and Facebook
I'm sitting in cafés with the panickers, the terrified and the lonely.
I know there is plenty to panic about.
I'm staying six feet away
chatting to the old man with the stroke in his arm and his leg.
How are you? he asks. I'm good, I answer.
I'm watching the surprise in his droopy eye
and his lopsided smile.

I'm talking to the German Hare Krishna, who owns the café,
and asking her how she copes with everyone coming in
and eating their anxiety and leaving saliva on the plates.
They're just stimulated by all of this, she says, but I have Krishna
and I will be all right.

Level 2

I'm waking up at five in the morning and I'm thinking maybe
Jacinda has become my Krishna
Hare Jacinda
Rama Primeminiscinda
I take her picture down and light my incense to nothing at all.

I'm asking my eighty-six-year-old mother to ring me half an
hour before she comes into the same room as
me and my daughter, so I can disinfect:
the light switches and the door knobs and the cupboard handles
and the fridge door and the microwave door and the knife-
drawer handle and the taps and the dishwasher door and the
bench and the tabletop and her dining-room chair and the
back of her chair and the landline phone and the TV remote
and the heat-pump remote
and then I walk quickly to the other end of the house and
disinfect the toilet and the flush button and all the light
switches and the taps and the empty towel rail.

I keep reminding my daughter:
Imagine Uncle is lying on the floor with his feet here and
his head there, that's how far you have to stay away from
Granny. I speak loudly to Mum (cos she's pretty deaf):
Stay away Mum, stay away.

Before my brother and my niece arrive for the last time,
my daughter is deep-frying panikeke
I say the word *dangerous* more than fifteen times
then I'm standing under the shower and forcing myself to
breathe
just leaving her with the boiling oil and standing under the
water and trying to breathe. I am just having a shower I am just
having a shower I am just having a shower.

I'm listening to Jacinda and clicking on her message to the nation
and the full media briefing she does afterwards
and the science woman with bright pink hair who shows us how
to wash our hands.
I am calling a briefing for my mother and daughter.

I am Jacinda
I'm plugging myself in to the TV and turning the volume up
loud enough that my daughter
has to cover her ears
and my mum can hear.
Are you ready, I ask them? Are you ready?

Level 3

Jacinda is saying tomorrow is lockdown
I know my daughter is out of sanitary pads and I'm not sure
if the taxis will keep running, so, I'm going to Wainoni
Pak'nSave with six zillion other people.
Jacinda told us to shop normally.
I'm telling myself: Shop normally shop normally shop normally
I'm forcing myself to buy one packet of toilet paper
and four cans of baby beetroot. A woman is taking photos of all
the different kinds of sanitary pads to send to her daughter.
She steps back and bumps into me. I'm trying not to freak out,
I'm forcing myself to walk slowly around the supermarket
walk slowly walk slowly walk slowly.

I'm going back to the health and beauty aisle and searching for
Rescue Remedy and not finding it
I see a guy I met on Tinder ages ago and didn't sleep with
and he says, Well, how do you tell the story?
and gives me a look as if it is a thing that neither of us

could know, as if it is a thing perhaps no one could know.
In the carpark a couple of young bogans
stick their heads out of the car window
and cough as loud as they can, laugh and drive off.

I'm reading what the microbiologist has said about
disinfecting.
You have to let it sit for ten minutes
or you're just moving the bacteria around.
I thought I was doing a good job keeping my mum safe.
I thought I was keeping her safe, so if she does die,
at least I will know I did all the right things
but I've just been moving it around.

Level 4

I'm listening to the bugle call in the kitchen.
Jesus isn't coming back or Armageddon
or even the end of Level 4
but here is the moment of silence, so I stop
whatever ten-minute meal I am making
and remember those who have fallen: the Anzacs and the Covid
cluster down the road at the Rosewood Rest Home.

How to get an abortion

When I take the *Broadsheet*s out of their museum boxes, the covers are familiar. I open one and brush my thumbs over the pages. The newsprint is velvety. I think of the strange little patch of downy fur at the base of my newborn baby's back. I put my face to the magazine and breathe in. It smells as sweet and musty as the inside of my mother's room.

<>

This is where she keeps things not meant for my eyes. Large white sanitary pads, the strange plastic-lace undies with elastic loops meant to hold the pads in place – I try them on. Her diary in her bedside drawer – I read it. I learn, in the tiny pages, the job Mum disappears to all day is hard, that it makes her eyes hurt, that we don't have enough money, that she's worried. In her room she also keeps a pile of *Broadsheet*s. I sit on her floor because I am 'sick'. I study the *Broadsheet*s carefully. I am eleven years old.

In the backyard while she digs out potatoes, I tell my mother I'm NEVER getting married. I am watching her marriage bow her over. And soon it will explode and rip through all of us like Beirut.

In the next few years Mum will tell me about the backstreet abortion and her aunty who performed it for her in 1959. And how her aunty went to prison for seven years when a later one, for someone else, went wrong.

Sitting on Mum's bedroom floor, looking through the *Broadsheet*s, I come across a naked woman lying on the floor, legs open, red blood pouring from her. I learn there about coat hangers. I wonder about the mechanics of this: I know the naked woman

77

has to get the coat hanger up inside herself somehow. But how does she hook the baby out? How does she know how to steer blind? And then, I see the puncture and the rip. And the blood that won't stop.

I flinch and I flinch for forty years.

<>

If you can afford it, go to Australia.
If you can't:
1. The gin and hot bath method.
2. Epsom salts.
3. Quinine.
4. Take 600 milligrams of vitamin C two times a day for five days, at the time period is due.
5. Insert thin sharp object into the uterus (the coat-hanger method).
6. Force soap solution, caustic soda or other harsh liquids into the uterus (my great aunty's method).
7. Suck out the contents of the uterus with a vacuum cleaner.

<>

In the last pile of *Broadsheet*s, in the last issue, I come to a photo. It is her. The woman. She reaches across forty years, into my mother's bedroom, into my eleven-year-old chest, where she has been all this time. I contract and open and expand.

She is in a small photo, bottom right-hand corner. She is on a placard in a demonstration in my hometown. Women gather around her. The curator tells me later this is a famous image. I don't know this. This is eleven-year-old me, on the bedroom floor, the scents of my mother around me. And her.

She is lying in a bathroom doorway, feet facing me, pigeon-toed. She is white, as white and as soft as my mother. The floor is dark and cold, her head is on the side, her arms are tucked up under her, her top half is almost peaceful, as if she might just be sleeping. In the foreground there are newspapers and tubing. An eight-shaped twist of dark tubing, like an egg timer or infinity. On her left leg there is a dark towel. Or maybe it is a blood-soaked towel, draped across the back of her white thigh. The scary bleeding out between the wide open vee of her legs – her final vanishing point.

There is no coat hanger. No blood-red. It is black and white, this picture. *Broadsheet* didn't come in colour. But what I have not misremembered across this long vā is her loneliness, her shocking bleeding-out-ness, her poor white naked body on the cold floor. I never forgot that. I never forgot that.

Prayer

I pray to you Shoulder Blades
my twelve-year-old daughter's shining like wings
like frigate birds that can fly out past the sea where my father lives
and back in again.
I pray to you Water,
you tell me which way to go
even though it is so often through the howling.
I pray to you Static –
no, that is the sea.
I pray to you Headache,
you are always here, like a blessing from a heavy-handed priest.
I pray to you Seizure,
you shut my eyes and open them again.
I pray to you Mirror,
I know you are the evil one.
I pray to you Aunties who are cruel.
You are better than university and therapy
you teach me to write books
how to hurt and hurt and forgive,
(eventually to forgive,
one day to forgive,
right before death to forgive).
I pray to you Aunties who are kind.
All of you live in the sky now,
you are better than letters and telephones.
I pray to you Belt,
yours are marks of Easter.
I pray to you Great Rock in my throat,
every now and then I am better than I am now.
I pray to you Easter Sunday.
Nothing is resurrecting but the water from my eyes
it will die and rise up again

the rock is rolled away and no one appears
no shining man with blonde hair and blue eyes.
I pray to you Lungs,
I will keep you clean and the dear lungs around me.
I pray to you Child,
for forgiveness, forgiveness, forgiveness.
I will probably wreck you as badly as I have been wrecked
leave the ship of your childhood, with you
handcuffed to the rigging,
me peering in at you through the portholes
both of us weeping for different reasons.
I pray to you Air,
you are where all the things that look like you live
all the things I cannot see.
I pray to you Reader,
I pray to you.

Not horror porn

I walked the medieval streets of Aleppo past two women in tight fitting gloves and heavy hijabs who lifted them to get a better look at me. I followed them deep into the jowls of the market and watched them finger lipstick-red lace G-strings, hold them up, stretch them out as far as they would go. I wondered what G-string size the two were and made a note to return to the stall and see if there was any sexy underwear that would fit me.

I was cruised by a man in an early-model cream Mercedes. He put his head out the window and whistled as I walked down an empty street in the late afternoon, somewhere near Palmyra. Then he drove away. Later the Mercedes circled back around. It stopped and the man got out and walked some way towards me, not too close but close enough for me to hear his apology.

I slept on Manal's bedroom floor for a month. I met her in a café in Damascus, she was smoking like a 1930s movie star. Her mother and two sisters slept in the lounge. I watched them roll cabbage leaves with rice and things I couldn't guess at. It took hours. Manal's mother didn't smile or speak to me. Her little sister pointed out the window and over the wall at the school with the ten-storey-high head and shoulders picture of al-Assad smiling down. She pointed at the concrete playground and told me about the training she did with her classmates every day, waiting for the Israelis to come. What will you do if they come? I asked. Kill them, she told me in her gentle pre-teen voice.

I walked the sunny streets of Damascus behind two police-men big as Samoan wrestlers. They strolled with their pinkies linked, much like Samoan boys or lovers would. There between the cobblestones a baby sativa grew untrampled and I saved it from their boots. Later, in the only town where the people still spoke in the tongue of Jesus, I sat in a stone circle with my sloe-eyed friends and rolled that tiny joint. I laughed with them and breathed in their beauty like it was something that couldn't last.

Race Riot

This is any one of them
Redfern or Ferguson or Eden Park
or the Pak'nSave carpark.
We are gathering anywhere

in a monastery or a high school or a real-estate agent's
we are planning everywhere
and I am still afraid.

Everyone armours up: cardboard inside their clothing
beaten out tin drums and strapping.
No one has thought of helmets.

The black boys change my mind
they are getting on with business
I pad up and take jackets from their hands

stuff them up my jumper
till I look like a blow-up sumo wrestler.
All the girls and all the boys are browner than me

blacker and more political and braver.
There is a sign saying *Heart* or it could be *HART*
I don't want to be batoned.

We march out, the whites behind the cordons
watch with those angry alabaster looks
raise their hands to point. It will truly serve us right.

Ten Eighty

Trying to see you, my eyes grow confused.
Behind you is something huge,
not a friendly thing like a fruit-bat
but a 50-foot thing made of smoke.
Something that floats up behind you when you say
My nigger will carry my bag
and laugh cos it's just a joke and we've been friends for years.

Trying to hear you, my ears grow confused
when you say, *Bloody Chink kids are taking over the school.*
Well, you know what I mean. Cos we've been having these
coffee mornings with the other mums
and it's all in good fun, for years.

Trying to speak to you, my throat grows confused
cos I've been swallowing 1080 poison pellets,
slow-release every day for years.
When I open my mouth, smoke comes out
the choking kind, the can't-breathe kind
the kind that lynch my words out of me.

So, when I try to answer you
I say nothing.

Unity (ii)

Dear Tusiata

On behalf of everyone at Unity Books
accept my full apologies
for the incidents you describe
for the incidents you describe
for the incidents you describe
you describe
you describe
you describe
please accept my full apologies
for any staff behaviour which you feel was racist
which you feel was racist
which you feel was racist
which you feel was racist
you feel
you feel
you feel
you feel was racist.

Our work here requires that we
prevent and deal with shoplifting
which amounts to over $20,000
a year, every year.

You feel shoplifting / $20,000 / a year / every year /
you feel shoplifting / shoplifting / shoplifting / shoplifting/
you feel $20,000 / $20,000 / $20,000 / $20,000 /
you feel every / every / every / every /
racist full apology / racist full apology / racist full apology.
Needless to say, this part of our job is the part we like least.

Yours sincerely,

How to be in a room full of white people

See	the huge room
Count again	the brown and black people in the room
Count again	to one or two or maybe three
Count again	to only you
Breathe	in onetwothreefourfivesixseveneightnine / hold /
Breathe	out onetwothreefourfivesixseveneightnine

<>

Listen	to white people talk about _____ and _____ and _____
Listen	to white people talk about writing
Listen	to white people who are writing as black men and black women
Hush	for prize-winning white people talking
Listen	to white people who are painting dead, black bodies with bullet holes
Listen	to white people say they don't know why they are painting dead, black bodies with bullet holes, but their art-school tutors are encouraging them to keep going

<>

Hear	white people pause before they miss the word they used to use
Hear	the tiny-tiny pause
Hear again	white people say *diversity*
Wonder	if you could unscrew that word like a lid, what might be inside the jar

<>

Listen to white people call you the name of the other brown
      woman writer
again
Repeat your name for white people who ask you to repeat your
      name
again
Listen to white people say: That's such a beautiful name, what
      does it mean?
again

<>

Listen to white people say: I went to Some-oh-wa on my
      holiday, I didn't stay in Up-peer, I stayed on Siv-vie-
      ee, it's traditional, they haven't lost their culture like
      the Mour-rees, I stayed in the village, everyone was so
      authentic
Listen to white people say: What do your tattoos mean?
      But do they have a meaning?
      But were they done the traditional way?
      We saw the proper ones – you have to be a chief to have
      them
Hear   white people say: My daughter has a tribal tattoo, it
      looks really similar. Celtic
again

<>

Hear   white people say: I own a dairy, the Hori kids steal the
      blue lighters and the red lighters
Listen to white people say: Crips and Bloods
Listen to white people say Hori again and look at you
again

88

Listen	to white people say: Well, *you'll* know what I mean?
Listen	to this in your head for weeks
Listen	to this in your head for weeks

<>

See	white people clasp a brown hand
Hear	white people mispronounce te reo
again	
Listen	to white people talk about their roots and their discovery
Listen	to white people talk about their research and their discovery and the discovery of their great-great-great-great
Listen	to what funding white people have applied for again, now they have whakapapa

<>

Watch	white people watch you as you enter
Wonder	if you'll have to empty your bag
again	
again	
again	
Breathe	in / onetwothreefourfivesixseveneightnine / hold /
Breathe	out / onetwothreefourfivesixseveneightnine
Breathe	when you leave and then feel so angry that you walk back in and walk around
again	
Pretend	to white people that you're not watching them watch you
again	
Watch	white people's eyes follow you when you leave
again	

<>

Watch	white people startle when you use the words *white people* together
Listen	to white people tell you they don't like being lumped together like that
Watch	white people when black and brown people are killed again because they are black and brown people
Hear	white people say: It's hard to be white too
Listen	to white people say: I feel culturally unsafe
Listen	to white people say: I'm a woman of colour, white's a colour
Listen	to white people say: I don't see colour
Listen	to white people say something about the human race and something about we're all the same and that all lives matter
again	
again	
again	

<>

Try	to reframe it
again	
Try	not to sound so negative
again	
Try	to stick your fingers down your throat and vomit up the poison pellet
again	
again	
again	
Try	to say something positive at the end of this poem, so you don't come across as the angry brown woman
again	
	writing about the things that white people don't want to be true.

Some notes for critics

1. Yeah, sometimes my poems are dark
2–5. Get over it
6. Angry
7. Check your pulse
8. You might be dead
9. I could write about landscape but it fucken bores me
10. Monet drew heaps of pictures of lily ponds
11. If I made references to the *Iliad* (or the like) you'd know what I was on about
12. Lay-ers
13. Samoan legends
14. It's not rocket science
15. Google it
16. Some writers don't include glossaries
17. I used to be a high school ESOL teacher
18. I'm nice like that
19. You still don't know what fale aitu means, ay?
20. Nope, not spirit house
21. Hahaha (that's a clue)
22. No?
23. Google it
24. Imagine you read three Pacific women's poetry collections. Would you:
25. Review them all together?
26. Use references from African-American culture?
27. (Or something from 'world' literature that you did your MA on?)
28. Be dragged towards the word *exotic* with the force of a giant moon?
29. Now, imagine three Pākehā men's collections – what would you do with those?
30. Put your hands up
31. If you are white.

FA'AFETAI LAVA

E momoli atu ma le agaga fa'afetai i le paia ma le mamalu i nai uso ma tuagane aemaise o e na lagolagoina si a'u taumafaiga ma le fa'asoaina lenei fa'amoemoe e ala i lenei tusi.

Dad, for your hand always on my shoulder. Mum, for always letting me tell my truth. Sepela, for your unending alofa.

Selina Tusitala Marsh, for your unfailing friendship and alofa, the daily conversations that get me through life, and self-help books and poetry. Cuz Victor Rodger for always having my back (and front and sides). Sis Hinemoana Baker, alofa tele to you and afio mai to *Funkhaus*. My poetry sisters Kate Camp, Maria McMillan, Stefanie Lash, Anne-Marie Te Whiu and Paula Green for reading early versions of some of these poems. Marty Smith for reading and giving feedback on the manuscript. Bernadette Hall for finding me when I was a closet scribbler, publishing my first poem and mentoring me for the last two decades. Ali Cobby Eckermann for surviving and writing and making us all braver. My Fika āiga: Danielle O'Halloran, Ana Mulipola, Faumuinā Maria Ifopo, Tanya Muāgututi'a, Jess Marama, Sarah Maindonald, Stephanie Oberg, Grace Vanilau for doing what only Pacific creative sisters can do for each other. Uso Khye Hitchcock and Nina Oberg for creating short writers' residencies at their respective exhibitions: *Making Space* at CoCa and *Vā Oceans Between* at Tūranga. Ana Mulipola, Jason Tiatia, Sarah Maindonald, Raina Kingsley, Urupikia Minhinnick for advice with gagana Sāmoa and te reo Māori. Fergus Barrowman and the team at VUP for your tautoko, which has included visiting me in hospital after seizures at writers' festivals. Ashleigh Young, for your patient and peerless editing. And to Pati Solomona Tyrell for creating the most kick-ass book cover ever!

NOTES

p.5: The epigraphs are from DeRay Mckesson, *On the Other Side of Freedom: The Case for Hope* (Viking, 2018) and Thomas Pynchon, *Gravity's Rainbow* (1973, Viking).

p.9: The Hawai'ian names in '250th anniversary of James Cook's arrival in New Zealand' refer to people involved or related in some way to the killing of James Cook. The poem includes the names of ships that Cook captained or worked on.

p.13: 'Listening to Tame' is a found poem. The source is Tame Iti's onstage interview at Womad 2018.

pp.19–20: St Barbara Company Ltd is an Australian goldmining company. Simberi is an island in the Tabar group in Papua New Guinea. Gorgor leaves are used by the indigenous people to signify a warning.

p.21: The 1918 influenza was brought to Sāmoa on a New Zealand passenger boat. The virus killed 22 per cent of Sāmoa's population. 'Shirley Boys' refers to Shirley Boys High School, 'Villa' to Villa Maria College.

p.25: 'Martin Luther King Day' is a found poem. The source is MLK NOW, a celebration to honour Martin Luther King, held in Harlem on 18 January 2020. This poem includes quotes from the spoken and written works of Martin Luther King, Barbara Jordan, Albert Einstein, John Lewis, Marcus Garvey, Ta-Nehisi Coates, Rep. Alexandria Ocasio-Cortez, Marshawn Lynch and The Holy Bible. Apologies for any references I may have missed.

p.31: 'Massacre' refers to the Christchurch massacre of 15 March 2019. Parihaka and Ruatoki refer to historical and contemporary military/police armed raids on Māori settlements.

p.35: 'Man in the wheelchair' is largely a found poem. The source is an onstage talk on Islam by Fareed Ahmed after the Christchurch massacre.

pp.61–65: The three 'FafSwag Spell' poems were written in response to the performance work of FafSwag (a Queer Indigenous arts collective) during the *Making Space* exhibition. La Chana Antonia Santiago Amador is a legendary flamenco dancer.

pp.67–69: 'Blacking out the Vā' (i–iii) refers to the legends of Taema and Tilafaiga and Samoan tatau. These poems were created by blacking out words from Albert Wendt's seminal essay 'Tatauing the Post-Colonial Body', originally published in *Span* 42–43 (April–October 1996): pp. 15–29.

p. 77: An earlier version of 'How to get an abortion' was comm-issioned by the Auckland Writers Festival.

p.85: The first line of 'Ten Eighty' is borrowed from the poem 'Therapy' in *The Black Unicorn* (1978) by Audre Lorde. Fa'afetai tele lava to Mark Vanilau for the conversation that inspired this poem.